TONJA WARING

"I am so fortunate to have met Tonja and have the opportunity to receive her coaching. She is so easy to talk to and work with. She surprised me with new ideas and approaches which have been of great benefit to me in my business and in living the best all-around life. I recommend her coaching to everyone interested in having more success in business by focusing on what brings you joy."

~ Rita C.

"The two major strengths Tonja consistently exhibits are that of Coaching/Mentoring and Business Development. Tonja has demonstrated a solid ability to coach/mentor others through whatever obstacles they face and has helped them develop and implement actions that will achieve their goals. This successful skill set is the result of excellent listening skills and the ability to empathetically immerse herself in their situation. Tonja excels in business development because of her high energy and positive nature. She accepts challenges and is determined to present nothing less than the winning scenario in every project she takes on."

~ James R.

"Tonja is an excellent coach! She is full of joy and enthusiasm for her work and so good at transferring that to her clients. She truly listens and supports her clients to create what they are looking for. I would highly recommend her to any person or business."

~ Connie D.

"I have known Tonja for over 15 years and have worked with her on several occasions. Tonja is remarkable, insightful, and intuitive. She often is able to help me to articulate what it is that I want expressed and then develops the best means by which to do that. Her work is stellar. She performs on time and with accuracy. Certainly, I will work with her again and again."

~ **Bonnie H.**

"I have known Tonja for over 17 years. Tonja is an independent thinker, a trustworthy individual, self-determined, reliable and very creative. I have seen her operate successfully as an entrepreneur and as part of different organizations. She can be counted on to bring her creative skills to make things happen. On a more personal level, Tonja is someone that can re-invent herself to adapt and to accomplish goals that not always are predictable. She is an outstanding human being, cordial, intelligent, committed to transforming anything in herself and the outside circumstances to accomplish her vision. Tonja is an extraordinary leader and a magnificent friend."

~ **Viviana S.**

"Tonja is one of the most dynamic and talented women that I have ever met! The enthusiasm that she has for her work and the people with whom she does business is admirable. It is no wonder that Tonja is a successful coach, bringing together her ability to see essential needs/connections combined with her genuine care for the best interest of those involved. Having been on the receiving end of her gifts on several occasions, I can attest that Tonja is an inspiration!"

~ Mark H.

"I met Tonja Waring while attending the Manifesting Prosperity Clubs™. She is an amazing woman who leads by example. I found a mentor and friend in Tonja. She truly believes in people, and I have not met anyone so giving and so honest. She is a wonderful person, business professional and dedicated mother."

~ Angelica G.

"Tonja is an incredibly succinct personality that emulates freedom and peace for those whom she touches with her work. Her professionalism abounds, and I have had the privilege to learn from her and transform my thinking and behaviors to new levels personally. I am grateful to know the peace of manifesting and programming positivity to the energies within my life. I recommend Tonja to anyone, corporately or privately, to receive the pathway she provides towards true transformation."

~ **Bonnie B**.

"Tonja Waring was our featured Guest Speaker at the last Awesome Women event in Bloomington, Minnesota. The purpose of Awesome Women is to develop, encourage and promote women's voices. Tonja shared her voice of wisdom and inspiration as she took us on a journey through her losses and showed us how her vindication and perseverance paid off. She is a living example for many of us who move from despair to hope. We were in awe at the spark of motivation that led her to initiate several entrepreneurial endeavors leading to multiple streams of income. We are very grateful to have the charismatic speaking ability of Tonja, and many women in our gathering learned a great deal about themselves. Tonja was an awesome example for all of us to follow."

~ **Lynn K**.

THE POWER
OF MANIFESTING

---

6 Secrets to Create, Manifest
& Get What You Want

---

by Tonja Waring

Manifest Publishing

TABLE OF CONTENTS

ABOUT TONJA WARING

Tonja Waring is The Manifesting Mindset™ Consultant for CEOs, entrepreneurs, and industry leaders. She is gifted at positioning and aligning leaders with their vision for measurable results.

Tonja has sold well over $50 million on TV, was a top infomercial host in 2012, is a best selling author, and owns multiple companies. Her greatest love is being the mother of three teenagers.

Tonja's success took off when the Manifesting Process™ was revealed to her by her Divine Guidance Team over the course of a year. This fundamental awareness of how to manifest with deliberate accuracy completely changed her life.

She literally went from being denied welfare and deeply depressed on the couch to being seen on national TV over 150 times a day. She also co-authored one of the most profitable newspaper ads ever written that appeared in *The New York Times*, *The Wall Street Journal* and *USA Today*.

Tonja is an unwavering advocate for our youth and entrepreneurialism. She has held a few corporate employee positions, but always has had at least one business of her own operating simultaneously since she was 16 years old.

She firmly believes strengthening our free market enterprise system will restore our middle class and liberate our poor, not only in the USA, but in every country around the world.

Tonja received the National Association of Entrepreneurs' Influencer – Making a Difference award in 2016. She believes that each of us possesses what we need to be everyday world changers. We are here with a purpose to make a difference, and if we would simply follow our burning desires, that purpose would be revealed and we would be growing towards our greatest human potential.

Her most recent undertaking, Grounds for Joy, is a social profit, online coffee company, where 50% of its profits impact youth and their parents by providing necessities like food, water, clothing and shelter. They also encourage independence through business, leadership education and spiritual awareness.

MANIFESTING
FENG SHUI

"All children are artists. The problem is how to remain an artist once he grows up."

~Pablo Picasso

Being natural born artists/creators, all children know how to manifest and given we were all children once, we have to assume that each of us knows how to manifest at some level.

Yes, even you!

The problem is that we forget many things as we grow up and manifesting is one of them.

There really are no "secrets" to manifesting; if there was a secret, I would say it is to remember what you already knew how to do and to gain conscious mastery in manifesting so that you never again forget how.

First, know that you are a natural born manifestor. Accept this as fact, embrace it and have fun with it. If you feel like you have lost this ability, simply ask that it be restored. You'll learn why this helps in the following chapters.

Watch any child and you will see their joy and their ability to create what they desire out of virtually nothing. I'm sure you know a child or two who are masters at getting what they want.

However, as we grow up and mature, we lose mastery of that ability for whatever reasons. But it doesn't matter so much as to why we lost the ability, what matters is that now we are ready to remember how to manifest and we can have lots of fun with it.

✳ ✳ ✳

My fascination with manifesting began in 1998 when I discovered an ancient Chinese practice known as feng shui. Feng shui is a science and an art that can be used to design environments for the greatest success in our finances, health, and relationships. It is about aligning everything in our home and office for the best energy flow which in turn impacts our overall quality of life.

There are nine life areas to play with: Prosperity, Fame and Reputation, Partnership, Family, Health, Children/Creativity, Self-Knowledge, Career and Helpful People/Travel. Playing with feng shui and making adjustments in these nine life areas can be a bit like a chess game.

I was pregnant with my daughter at the time and also planning to have a home birth; I wanted everything to be just right. Someone then suggested I looked into feng shui; which I had never even heard of before. One day, while at a Barnes and Nobles bookstore, I was drawn to the feng shui section. As I flipped through the pages of several books, I immediately fell in love with feng shui. It felt like I already knew everything that I was reading. It made perfect sense to me.

Excited, that very day, I bought 12 books (over half the books in the feng shui section at the time) and I read them cover-to-cover in the span of two to three weeks.

Applying what I'd learned, I made adjustments to my own home and without me saying anything, my friends noticed. Soon after, they began asking me to do feng shui consultations at their homes. Even though I was a natural, I wasn't 100% sure I was doing everything 'right', so I decided to take a feng shui course. I ended up taking a two-year apprenticeship with advanced studies in feng shui.

I consulted for several years in both homes and businesses. Sometimes, the results were immediate, and sometimes they took longer to manifest. However, there was always a shift that took place. It was fascinating and still is to me today.

There are several forms of feng shui, and Black Sect Feng Shui is what I studied the most. Black Sect Feng Shui was developed by Grandmaster Professor Thomas Lin Yun who transformed ancient Buddhism and Chinese philosophies to be adapted to the modern life and modern challenges of the West.

He established the Four Guiding Principles that I have lived by ever since I learned them.

- ☯ Everything is energy.
- ☯ Intention is most important.
- ☯ Your space reflects your life.
- ☯ Use nature as your model.

Intention is an incredibly powerful tool that each of us can easily use. However, most of us are not clear on our intention. It has been said that the most difficult question we will ever ask ourselves is, "What do I want?"

Once we know what we want, it is easy to set an intention and manifest that.

Manifesting Feng Shui Success Story

My greatest feng shui success story was with a couple who wanted to build a $500 Million power plant. Their home was beautiful, and they had a few businesses.

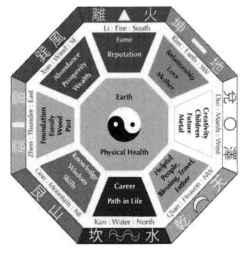

For over a year, they were getting all kinds of publicity: Radio, TV, Newspaper, etc. but no investors for the deal. When I looked at their floor plan, I could see that their Fame and Reputation area was on FIRE! Which, is awesome because they were getting lots of publicity.   However, their Prosperity area was completely missing.

We did a simple and affordable cure, and about one week after the consultation, they received $100 Million in funding which was the seed money they needed to get the project going.

We just had to get their prosperity corner right, and we did!

To learn more about feng shui, you can go to my website www.ManifestingFengShui.com.

I've always known it is possible to manifest. However, I was not having much luck with it for myself. Sometimes I noticed it was really easy and other times, no matter what I tried, it just wouldn't happen at all. I was totally frustrated with myself more than anything else because I wasn't happy in my life as I wanted to be; I wanted good things for myself and my children. I must have watched *The Secret* at least 50 times, but it didn't seem to help much.

In fact, when the real estate crashed in 2007/2008, I lost most everything with it. I went through foreclosure. I got divorced. I couldn't find a job. Yada, yada, yada. I was barely hanging on mentally. I had three little kids who were looking at me like, "What is wrong with you? Why are you acting like this?"

Yes, I was "trying" to get a job. I put out 200 resumes with only one interview. There were 30,000 other real estate agents just like me looking for work. And, I'm sure I came off like the mess that I was.

Then one day, I had this crazy idea. Actually, it wasn't a crazy idea at all. For the first time in a long time, I was crystal clear on what I wanted. I was perfectly clear that I was an amazing person and that I deserved to ask for and receive what I wanted. I literally had such a moment of clarity, that I stood up off the couch and told God, "Look, God. I am smart, I am beautiful, and I am talented. Would you please bring me something that is worthy of who I am?"

I thought to myself, *I want something I could sell and make decent commissions off of.* I wanted…no, IT HAD TO BE something I believed in 100%. I wanted to sell a product that I believed in because I wanted complete integrity in the work I was going to do next.

I'm not even sure what I did after that, I probably went back to being depressed on the couch. I really didn't know what I was going to do, I just knew what I wanted and being clear about that part, somehow, made me feel better.

About a week and a half later, I received a call from a friend who recommended that I come to work with a small pillow company that he had been working with the last few weeks. "They need you," he said.

I was feeling so unwanted at this point that the possibility of working with a company that needed me, was encouraging. I met with the owner of the company, Mike Lindell at a restaurant, and he encouraged me to come in and meet with his CEO. When I went in for my interview, I saw exactly what to do for them in my mind's eye. I received a blueprint of sorts and was shown exactly what to do.

They hired me as a contractor.

It wasn't a great, high-paying job by any means but it was a job. The first thing I did was to improve their banner design for their tradeshow. Next, I wrote a story for their website. Their sales went up as I rewrote sales materials and worked on the sales pitch. I started driving all over the Midwest to sell pillows at tradeshows and fairs. It was hard work, really hard work: I stood on cement for three days and drove for two days each week; I had to be away from my children, and I hated that. But, in many ways, I needed that, too. I cried a lot but I also felt better about myself and what I was doing.

Using feng shui, I designed the set up my booth and was pretty successful at what I was doing. Life was looking up for me.

A few months later, I decided to enroll in a year-long program to become a certified Law of Attraction coach. I signed up because I was willing to pay for the 'title' to be a *certified* Law of Attraction Coach but what I didn't know was that it was a real live coaching program. I thought it was going to be a bunch of videos I could watch whenever, take a little online test here or there and then I could call myself a *certified* Law of Attraction Coach. But that wasn't the case.

After I enrolled, I learned that I had homework every week, plus a required attendance on coaching calls and group calls every week. I also had to have 70 hours of recorded coaching calls where I was the coach. These calls were going to be critiqued and evaluated before I could become *certified.* (Yes. I should have asked a lot more questions before I enrolled!)

I had no idea if it was even possible for me to complete the class; I was already traveling four or five days a week where cell phone use was sketchy, had three young children to care for when I was home and all of a sudden, it seemed almost impossible. But, I knew that I had to do it. I wanted to learn how to manifest for real and it didn't even matter if I passed the class or not. All I wanted to learn how to get what I wanted.

THE
MANIFESTING PROCESS™

"Believe in what you want so much that it has no choice but to materialize."

~Karen Salmansohn

The classes confirmed a lot of what I already knew, and taught me where I was off course in manifesting. I loved the classes and my calls with my teammates each week; they were so encouraging and accommodating to my schedule and I couldn't have done it without them.

I was spending at least 10 hours a week driving. While I was drove, I was began to hear the whisper of my Divine Guidance Team even more and over time, The Manifesting Process™ was revealed to me. I would receive inspired thoughts and thought-provoking questions from them. I was consciously asking my Divine Guidance team to help me better understand concepts like The Law of Deliberate Creation and The Emotional Guidance Scale, and then I would practice, study and discover what worked best for me.

Being mathematically inclined by nature, I worked with several steps, ideas and formulas until I discovered a succinct and efficient process to master manifesting. I boiled it down to six steps that I'm excited to share with you. The best part is that is simple and it works!

The Manifesting Process™

1. Get Clear on What You Want
2. Ask and It is Given
3. Surrender to that Higher Voice
4. Take Inspired Action
5. Receive to Overflowing
6. Celebrate Your Successes

❋ ❋ ❋

Manifesting is not just about creating more money in your life: it's about having your life as you design it; about listening to your desires and following that lead; and ultimately surrendering to that Higher Voice that leads you in the right direction.

There is so much more available to each of us than just money. In feng shui, the prosperity/abundance life area is denoted with the color purple. Purple is also the color of royalty.

Prosperity is about living a royal life; a life where you are designated as valuable just for being who you are.

Prosperity is about being prosperous in your health, your spirituality, your relationships and your emotions. It is about being able to create what you want when you want it.

Make a game out of what I'm about to teach you. See what you can manifest and share this information with your friends. Most of all, have fun!

Practice. Refine. Fix. Find your own flow.

I am going to share one tip with you before we get started. It is something I learned from Dr. Wayne Dyer. And, that is…

Don't tell anyone what it is that you want to manifest.

Just don't do it. That is your secret. Now, every rule has a rule for breaking the rule. *Did I just write that?* Anyway, if you feel inclined to tell someone because your Divine Guidance Team is urging you to do so, then go ahead and tell them. Just don't go telling everyone you know-- especially those closest to you.

I call the people closest to us 'Subconscious Saboteurs' when it comes to manifesting. Think of being connected to those in your inner circle with a rubber band; everyone is comfortable until someone stretches out and puts more pressure on everyone else.

We attracted everyone and everything to us at our current vibration.

When we start to vibrate at a different level, they want us to stay where they are. Subconsciously, they don't know why they feel the way they do which can sometimes cause them to get in the way of our growth. They want to be supportive, but they are uncomfortable. If you stay in your higher vibration, the vibration that you are needing to be in to manifest what you want, you will watch them eventually begin to shift to your level.

Though this process may create some chaos with those close to you, in time you will all be in alignment again. Be willing to accept that some of them may go off and find others who are at the same vibrational level as they are. Remember not to take it personally. It is part of the process and usually it's for the best.

Manifesting Secret #1

GET CLEAR ON
WHAT YOU WANT

"What we are today comes from our thoughts of yesterday, and our present thoughts build our life of tomorrow. Our life is the creation of our mind."

~Buddha

Knowing EXACTLY what you want is the first step in manifesting. Manifesting requires more than just 'wishful thinking':

I wish I felt better.
I wish I had a boyfriend.
I wish I had a better job.
I wish I could write a book.
And so on...

What happens with this type of thinking is that we say it with no real intention to have the thing that we want. We say it but we won't change one single thing about ourselves-- that won't manifest a darn thing!

When I say, "Get clear on what you want," I'm talking about the clarity of focus that comes with the desire to have something so much so that it nags your soul not to have it. Because of this, you actively will be thinking about--and seeking-- ways to get what you want. Your focus will be on what you desire to manifest. It could be the desire to go to college or to be married to someone who loves to travel as much as you

Join The Manifesting Mindset Mastermind

do. Whatever desire you have will resonate with every cell in your body and with your entire being.

Now, sometimes we desire something, but we aren't really focused on it because we have stuffed that desire down for so long that we aren't even aware of it. Or, we've given up almost every hope of having it, so we ignore it.

Ignoring our innate desire and wants is a recipe for illness. **We cannot ignore what we love or want without hurting ourselves.** We are born with that desire for a purpose: it is our life's blueprint, intended to pull us forward in the best direction. Each person knows what that is for themselves. It doesn't come from some other person.

Manifesting requires clear, focused intention of what you desire. I'm going to teach you how you can build your desires by listening to them and how to focus on what you really want. But, first you have to know what you want. If you don't know what you want, the rest of this book is useless. You cannot apply the next five steps without it.

Consider that when we know what we want, the Universe conspires to bring that to us. We don't have to know the how, we just have to know what we want.

In *The Alchemist*, Paulo Coelho, states that the most difficult question we ask ourselves is, "What do I want?"

"Clarity is the seed to prosperity."

~ Tonja Waring

Remember the Four Guiding Principles of Feng Shui? Now, let's take a deeper look at the first principle: **Everything is energy.**

Everything that exists on the planet in the physical is made of matter. Matter is universal. Everything physical is made up of the same type of energy: protons, neutrons and electrons. The only difference is the form of the matter. But, everything else is the same. This means that there are no boundaries to what you can manifest physically.

It is as easy to manifest a castle as it is a button. Everything is energy and energy is in unlimited supply to use for our creation. Your thoughts are energy. Your thoughts have the power to organize matter. It is imperative that you know what you want and FEEL what you want.

Now take a look at the second principle, **Intention is most important.** Intention focuses the energy so that matter can take form. Energy can be random, flowing, unorganized but intention organizes this energy, much like the tuning dial on a car radio can bring in a clear sound.

Think of the power of the laser beam. Most light is traveling in waves or is randomly scattered. The laser organizes light into a power force that can even cut steel! The clearer and more intentional we are about what we desire, the more powerful and focused our energy is to attract to us what we want.

So why do we have such a difficult time focusing on what we want?

Because we have an infinite supply of options available to choose from! We can create anything, we can choose anything and there are no right or wrong things to manifest. You can be like a kid in a candy store and have whatever you desire.

MANIFESTING TIP: Make a DAILY Habit of writing down what you want.

One of the best exercises to get crystal clear on what you want, is to start writing ideas and notions about what you want on a tablet—white paper with blue lines preferably. Make a daily habit of it.

If we take the time to engage ourselves in what we want and we start to see it in writing, over a little time, we get more and more clear on what it is that we really want. We may realize that what we thought we wanted may not be at all what we want…so, then we can take it off the list.

And for those things that we really do want, we begin to strongly desire them more. Keep writing down your ideas of what you'd like to do, be or have. Ask your Divine Guidance Team (angels, God, Jesus, deceased relatives, etc.) to clearly show you your desires and dreams. Ask for a bigger vision to be presented to you. Ask to remember what it really was that you wanted to do when you arrived here on this planet!

When you are out and about, start to see things you really like. Notice if you become envious and ask yourself why? What do you wish you had? What is the feeling you associate with what you desire that you wish you had? Become aware of how you want to FEEL.

What if you ask for something, receive it and realize that you don't want it? Don't worry about it! Just let it go and move on to what you really want.

Or, what if you love what you receive but then almost immediately you want something new? Don't worry about it either, we are meant to continually want more in our life.

Join The Manifesting Mindset Mastermind

What's Next?

Here is an incredible insight. You are never going to be 100% satisfied! That is good! That means you are alive and evolving! The moment we manifest what we want, there is something else or another life experience that we automatically will have a desire to have. It's how the human race and every animal on the planet evolves. It is the reason we know that the world will continue to get better and better. You can count on this.

Continually refine your list.

Allow yourself to dream and keep on dreaming. You will notice that your dreams will begin to expand. When you have a rather clear picture of what you'd like your life to be like, write your Dream Life Story in detail.

Think about a day in the future 18 months from now. (Write the date 18 months from today in the upper right hand corner.) Describe what you would like your ideal day to look like and feel like. Your subconscious mind is clear of the time available to manifest what you want. Almost anything you want to accomplish is possible in that time frame.

Don't expect to get clear in one sitting. This may take days or weeks to figure out. The important thing is to keep writing down your ideas. And, this is a really, really good time to hire a coach or engage in a mastermind with someone who thinks as big as or bigger than you do!

Goal Setting

According to Dave Kohl, professor emeritus at Virginia Tech, people who regularly write down their goals earn nine times more over their lifetimes than the people who don't. Yet, an overwhelming majority of Americans (80%) don't have goals.

A notorious Harvard study, uncovered that only 3% of people review their goals on a regular basis. This same study showed that the 3% who wrote down and reviewed their goals made more money than the rest of the 97%. So, if you truly want to manifest financial prosperity, start writing your goals down and review them regularly!

As far as the fact that 80% of Americans do not have goals—that explains to me why we have so many people sitting in front of the TV and/or wandering the malls aimlessly. If you don't have a goal or destination point, there is no real point in taking action outside of your comfort zone. You will not receive inspiration.

I believe one of the most positive things we can do for our kids is to help them get clear and excited about what makes them happy and help them to create a vision of what they want to achieve in their life with purpose. Let's teach them that they get to choose what they want to have happen in their life. Who are we to tell our kids they cannot do something or make them do something they really do not want to do?

Now, this doesn't mean that as parents we have to supply what they want for them. You are not the Universe. Teach them the Manifesting Process™. Let them know that the Universe is abundant and teach them how to tap into that--rather than your pocket book.

✭ Remember: You have within you the power to create anything you choose. Now, that doesn't mean everything. But, you can create anything you put your mind, spirit and intention to. That's pretty cool.

Strategies:
Clarify Your Intention

- What you focus on expands. Focus your attention on what you want and create a powerful intention to have it.

- Write down your intention in one or two sentences a few times a day in a notebook for at least nine days. Use blue lines on white paper.

- Write your intention in the shower with a dry erase marker. When you are in the shower, think about your intention. Visualize yourself having what you want. How will you feel when you have what you want?

- Let go of any attachment to how it is going to happen. The most important thing is to stay clear on what you want and review your intention/goals regularly!

- State your intentions in the positive. Rather than saying, "My intention is to not go into foreclosure..." instead, say something like, "My intention is to have a positive monthly cash flow of $2,000 or more by September 19, 2016."

- Here are a couple of other examples:
    - "My intention is to receive an 'A' in my social studies course."
    - "My intention is to have more than enough time, money and resources to do what I want, when I want.

Manifesting Secret #2

ASK FOR
WHAT YOU WANT

"Ask and it will be given to you; seek and you will find; knock and the door will be opened to you."

~ Matthew 7:7

Whether you are a believer or a nonbeliever, whatever we ask for is given. It is always given without fail.

We don't have to be smart enough, kind enough, or good enough. We don't have to do something in exchange for it. All we have to do is ask and it is given.

Once you are clear on what you want, the second step is to ask for what you want either out loud or in writing.

I have a Divine Guidance Team that I call on for assistance. I ask them to help. Asking for help from something bigger than myself seemed to open up communication in the form of what I often call the Higher Voice or 'whisper'.

Whatever your relationship with God or the Universe is or isn't, just ask. Even if you don't believe in a higher power, you can write down what you want in the form of Get Statements.

Get Statements

My business coach, Gary Barnes of Gary Barnes International, taught me how to write 'Get Statements' to get what I want. Things manifest so quickly it is amazing. These statements are about receiving, not doing.

First, develop six or seven sentences for things you want to receive, or 'get'. You write them in a short sentence from a place of receiving vs. making things happen. Keep them succinct and to the point because you will be writing these statements every day.

Also include a 'by when' date. Then you write them every day for at least 30 days. So many times, I have received what I wanted before the 30 days came, that I keep adding new things that I want to receive!

And, remember that it does take time to manifest, so don't get discouraged if what you want doesn't appear the moment you write it down! Make this fun, playful and easy.

Example:

I graciously receive $10,000 or more a month consistently starting June 6, 20XX.

My daughter will get braces by August 20, 20XX.

I have positive cash flow of $500 or more per month starting June 15, 20XX.

**Here is another fabulous idea
I learned from Gary.**

He taught me to set my end of the year mindset to December 15. Who wants to work over the holidays? **Plan to end your year early**. Good thinking!

at www.TheManifestingMindset.com

The first year I did this, I actually took time off from December 4 to December 12 to spend time with my parents when they visited. Then, my kids started their school vacation right after that. I spent most of the holidays with family. As an entrepreneur, this was the first time I had done that since my daughter was born 17 years earlier.

Here's what you do NOT want to write.

- I will <u>work hard</u> for $10,000 or more a month starting June 6, 20XX.

- I will <u>make</u> $200 more per month so my daughter will get braces by August 20, 20XX.

- I <u>don't want</u> to go into foreclosure.

Here's a snapshot of how writing Get Statements and/or Your Dream Life Story works, regardless of your beliefs.

Our brain is a deletion machine. We receive something like 3 trillion bits of information per second. (Ok, so how does anyone actually know this??) So, to be able to function with all this information that is bombarding us 24 hours a day nonstop, our brain cancels everything out except that which is familiar to us; things we see and experience on a regular basis.

Anything and everything we need to manifest what we desire is really all around us, all the time. We just don't recognize it, so we don't see it. Our brain simply deletes it. We only are aware of what we already know. We do not recognize anything that is out of the ordinary to us.

If you want to change your life and attract new things to you, you have to reprogram your brain to notice that which is alignment with what you want to manifest, not necessarily what you are familiar with.

That is exactly what Get Statements do. When we write down what we desire to receive, our brain experiences that kinesthetically through our writing and visually when we see the words on paper.

When we write Get Statements everyday, we are tricking our brain into recognizing things that we want before we have the experience of them. We can ask for $500 more per month, and then we will see an ad that offers $500 per month for something you would enjoy doing in exchange for it. Before our Get Statements, that same ad could be there, but we wouldn't necessarily see it. So, we feel like we are not getting what we want.

Now, that said, I've asked out loud for things that I have never written one sentence for, and it has shown up really, really quickly. And, I've come to the conclusion that when I've don't that, I have completely surrendered to faith. I realize that I no longer have the stamina within me to *make* it happen. When we surrender and ask for help, this opens the doors for our Divine Guidance Team to get to work for us, which it loves to do.

We have so much available to us that we don't take advantage of because we simply haven't known how to tap into it. My Divine Guidance Team talks to me all the time, and it is because I listen. I know they are here to help me. And, I can be stubborn and want to work hard even though I know I don't need to. Humans! We do make some things very, very difficult.

All I know is, be ready to receive what you ask for because it can show up really fast: a new home, a check in the mail, a new romance, a job offer, etc.

Sometimes, we miss it because we are not ready or willing to receive it just yet. We might think or say, "That was too easy. I can't just take it." Or, "I haven't even worked for it yet. What would people say if I just took it for myself?"

Sometimes what arrives is something we can use to get exactly what we want or it may be an inkling or internal nudge to do something out of our normal routine. If we aren't listening to our Higher Voice (or whisper or intuition) and following the directions, we may have a more difficult time receiving what we have asked for. Once you ask for something, tune in to your higher guidance and start to look for it. Pay attention!

The good news is that our Divine Guidance Team will persist at knocking on our door several times doing their best to get our attention to lead us towards what we want. But if we change our mind, or lose our focus, it may pass us by--which I suspect happens way more often than any of us are aware of or will admit to. Then we sit there waiting or give up, believing we never got what we asked for. Then we throw our hands up and say, "This manifesting stuff doesn't work!"

※ ※ ※

I was talking to a client who was considering leaving his wife. He told me he asked God for clear direction. He said he kept praying, and he wasn't getting any answer.

I questioned him, "Really, you don't get *any* answer? Or, do you get the answer, but it is not the answer you want?" He admitted that he did get an answer and he wasn't willing to follow through on what he knew was the right thing to do.

There is nothing too big or too small.

Ask. It is yours.

Ask for anything that you want.

Ask. It is yours.

Ask out loud.

Ask. It is yours.

When we ask out loud or on paper, the thought goes from our mind to our heart. When we ask out loud or on paper, we can feel inside our heart if what we asked for is a good fit for us. When we keep it all in our mind, it is a swirl.

Keeping our wants in our mind makes it challenging to know what is in alignment with us and what is not. Have you ever said something that sounded so right in your head, but the moment it left your lips you wish you could take it back?

Speaking out loud or in writing allows us the opportunity to get in resonance with what we desire to have in our life. If it doesn't sound right or feel right when we write it down or say it out loud, we can refine our request right then. It is easy to do.

Sometimes, I will ask out loud for something and when I actually hear it out loud, I think, "NO! Cancel, cancel!" Because I realize almost immediately that is not what I wanted. However, it is kind of a fun game to turn right around and clearly announce what it is that I do want.

Ten times out of 10 when you say something that doesn't feel right when you say it, you will have immediate clarity with what you DO want.

One day, when I was feeling overwhelmed in my business, I said out loud, "I wish things would slow down."

"NO!!! Cancel. Cancel!" I retracted, laughing.

In truth, I did not want my business to slow down! So, I refined my desire out loud, "What I really want are people who can help me expand my business in a flowing, fun and harmonious way."

When I thought about it further, I realized that what I really wanted was a personal assistant who lives close by. I wanted someone who could stop over when I needed to go over projects, but would spend the majority of time working at her home.

All of a sudden, I had this inspired thought to post on my Home Owners Association Facebook page a request for a personal assistant. It took about 60 seconds to post the ad, and I think she responded in less than two minutes. She lived on my street and was absolutely the best possible personal assistant I could have ever imagined! Thank you, my Divine Guidance Team, for giving me the idea and delivering the very best person to me!

Why not start today asking for *exactly* what you want?! If I can do it, you can do it!

I think some of our Divine Guidance Teams are snoozing because they are bored. They want to communicate with us, but we are too busy working hard to have what we want that we don't have time to listen. We don't use our angels enough! Once you start to get the hang of asking and receiving, asking and receiving, asking and receiving, there begins to be quite a flow that happens.

There is nothing too big or too small to ask for help. Whatever it is, they are willing to help you. I find that I now ask for lots of stuff. I ask for things like,

Dear God, I would love to drive a beautiful car that is a great fit for me.

I also ask for help with things, like:

Hey Angels, I could use your help finding my car keys...again.

(How many of you can relate to that one? Ha ha. I'm always misplacing things.) Within a few seconds, I will receive a nudge. I might have a thought to look for something else like a notebook, and instead, I find my car keys where I look for my notebook. It is kind of crazy, and I usually end up laughing.

My friends saw me do this one day, and thought I was crazy. Then, when they lost their car keys they decided they would try it and ask their angels to help find the keys. They called me excitedly telling me it worked! (Of course, it did.)

I have so much fun discovering more about how all this works. I enjoy playing with new ideas and trying different things. I find it fun to play with asking for things and watching them show up. Allow for the Universe/God/Angels/Source to answer your request in any way possible. Asking is the best way I know of to 'superpower' your life.

Get in the habit of asking
for what you want.

There is no rule saying you have to meet any certain requirements to have what you want because in truth, you already have everything.

You are a precious child of God. All you have to do is ask and it is given. That is a promise. When you fully understand this, it is natural to expect to receive exactly what you have asked for.

Strategy:
Ask for What You Want

There is power in asking out loud or putting your request in writing. When you ask out loud, you are telling your Divine Guidance Team to "Listen up! Bring it to me now. I am ready!"

You don't have to be bossy about it, but it does help to be firm. Imagine that everything you desire is simply waiting in storage locker for you. You were born with this storage locker full of goodies just for you! The moment you ask for something from your storage locker is like giving your ticket to the coat check person. Soon, they come back with your coat! The one you were expecting to receive. Nobody else has that ticket, just you! It takes some time to manifest. So, even if it takes a bit, be patient. It's coming!

And, you don't need to worry one little bit about someone going without because you were bold enough to ask for what you want. They have their own storage locker, too. Teach them how to ask, especially your kids. Do not become their manifestor. They can do it!

Write down at least 5 things you would like to "get" from the Universe in the next 18 months:

1.

2.

3.

4.

5.

Manifesting Secret #3

SURRENDER TO THAT HIGHER VOICE

"The greatness of a man's power is the measure of his surrender."

~ William Booth

Surrender.

It came to me in a moment when I had extinguished all hope of being able to dig myself out of my own hole. I had no job, no money and three little kids to feed. For a of couple weeks, I wondered if I should consider just giving up. It had never occurred to me to do that before. I was notoriously tenacious, upbeat, optimistic, strong, hard working, and resilient. But, nothing I was doing was working, and I just didn't have it in me to keep fighting.

I was also very prideful and never wanted to ask anyone for help. I was always the one helping everyone else. I'd rather die than ask for help.

I thought about having a nervous breakdown.

I know it sounds weird that I laid in my bed for a few days wondering if I could just check out mentally. You know, go over the edge. I visualized that if I had a nervous breakdown that then I wouldn't have to ask for help, some ambulance would take me away, and my parents would be called to take care of my kids. Most importantly, my pride would be saved. Then, and only then, could I not be blamed for my own failure. I would have a condition I could blame.

I knew without a doubt that my parents would take care of my kids. But, I also knew that it would leave my children with wounds that would never heal completely. I just couldn't do it.

Then, I laid on the floor in the sunshine for a few days trying to muster up enough energy to get moving. That wasn't working so well, either.

As I shared earlier, in a moment of inspiration, I finally did the only thing that made sense to do. I called out to God asking for help. At that moment, I had surrendered.

Surrendering is a terrifying moment immediately followed by glorious moment, or that's how it was for me. I know being so strong-willed, I suffered far more than I ever needed to! I could have given in and asked God for help long before I did. He was always there for me. Looking back, I can see that so clearly.

For several years, I taught the Manifesting Process™ without the 3rd Step: Surrender. Then, one day I was watching *Super Soul Sunday* with Oprah and

Join The Manifesting Mindset Mastermind

the guest talked about Surrender and what an incredible role that had played in his success in life. She commented that it played a significant role in her success as well. I knew immediately that it was indeed part of The Manifesting Process™.

To surrender is to ask that Higher Power to guide you and lead you. To surrender is to ask to be an instrument of some will other than your own. It is the action behind faith.

When I surrendered, this Higher Voice became more clear. I became better at listening and following directions. I became more peaceful and understanding. Following this Higher Voice lead me more directly on the path to my purpose and calling in life. It wasn't always easy. And, listening to that Higher Voice was not a guarantee of success.

Surrendering to that Higher Voice was an opportunity to experience things I wouldn't have otherwise had the chance to do in that particular timing.

When my friend told me about the job with the pillow company, my thought was that I didn't want to do it. I remember thinking, "Really God? You want me to sell a pillow with a guy who is just coming off a 30-year cocaine addiction?"

I heard, "Yes." Now, I know that this was not *my* idea to go work here. But, I knew that is what the Higher Voice was suggesting, and I could make my choice either way. The answer no matter how many times I asked and questioned, was to go and work for this company. So, I did. And, the rest they say is history.

Working with the pillow company, I became a top infomercial host, appeared as a guest on QVC over 30 times and wrote one of the most profitable newspaper ads ever written. That company grew from $500,000 to over $50 Million the two short years I worked there.

None of this was even an idea or opportunity on my radar. I had never been on television. However, I remember thinking that I would really love to be on TV. It was a couple weeks after that when I received a call that they would like me to be the host of the infomercial.

When we surrender, we allow our Divine Guidance Team to step in and show us an easier way. And, it can be really, really fun!

Strategy:
Surrender to that Higher Voice

The best way to surrender to a Higher Voice is to set your intention to surrender to a higher power. Have fun and allow yourself to be open to receiving guidance. If you get nudges to do something, do it. Become curious and see what the outcome is going to be.

Don't take it too seriously.

Play and go along with it. It does take practice. The more you listen and follow directions, the more directions you will receive. Like with any significant relationship, it's all about learning the best way to communicate.

If you receive a nudge to do something and ignore it, you will have a more difficult time establishing the relationship because you haven't really surrendered now, have you?

Most people who have surrendered ask God daily and even moment to moment for guidance. They literally turn their lives over to be used for the Highest Good. Of course, we always have the right to say,

"No", and I have. I do it by telling my Divine Guidance Team more of a 'not now'. Sometimes, I just don't want to listen and that is okay--but I don't ignore it. I'm very much aware of it yet I simply choose not to do what I'm hearing there is to do. Sound familiar? I can certainly see how we refer to divine guidance as Heavenly Father or Earthly Mother. It feels very much like going against what your parents want for you.

If you are finding it difficult to surrender and you want to surrender, simply go back to Manifesting Secret #2 and ask for what you want. Ask that you be shown how to surrender! Remember that anything we want, we can ask for.

Surrendering makes it easier for us to manifest more quickly; it is the shortcut to our desire.

Manifesting Secret #4

RECEIVE TO OVERFLOWING

"If you wish for light, be ready to receive light."

~ Rumi

If you have;

1. Gotten clear on what you want

2. Asked out loud for it and

3. Surrendered to that Higher Voice

Then now is the time to just say, "Yes!"

To 'realize' our manifestations, we must learn to fully receive. It is time to receive all of the great things that have been waiting for you. All you had to do was ask and get yourself out of the way.

The old adage that it is better to give than to receive is an untruth—perhaps one of the greatest untruths of our time.

If everyone is giving, who then is receiving? The answer is, no one. There is a natural flow of giving and receiving. Equal reciprocity.

Giving and receiving happen simultaneously so one cannot be better than the other. Unless we want to believe giving is better to make ourselves feel better, and then that would be our ego talking, not our Higher Voice.

When we receive to overflowing, only then can we give without a hint of resentment or reservation because our own cup is already overflowing.

Giving from a full cup is Divine Giving.

This is the purest essence of love--no one goes without. Everyone is taken care of in the divine flow of give and take.

Everything you desire is already yours. There isn't anything you could possibly want that hasn't already been designated for you, for your highest and best good. Remember, your storage locker is full. When we are at our highest and best, then the world receives the highest and best too.

Whenever you have the experience of not getting what you ask for, it is because you are not allowing yourself to receive it. In other words, you are resisting accepting it. Whether you are aware of it or not, you are not allowing it to come to you.

Maybe you think you haven't 'earned the right' to have it yet, so you want to work harder for it. Maybe you think what you've received should be a different shape or color. Or, maybe you think it should have come to you in a different chain of events somehow. We come up with all kinds of reasons to push great things away from us.

Sometimes, we aren't willing to let go of what we have that is not working for us so we can make room for something better that is coming to us.

Prosperity is your birthright. The Universe is infinite. You have an unlimited supply of energy with which to create. No matter how much you receive, you could never take so much that someone else would go without because everything you want and need is already yours.

I thought by the time I had become a top infomercial host and immersed myself in the study of Law of Attraction for an entire year, that I had pretty much handled everything I needed to be and remain prosperous. Unbeknownst to me, even after my success and moving my kids to Texas from Minnesota, I still needed to learn a lesson on receiving. I'm still learning. Receiving was one of the most difficult lessons for me.

One morning as I was driving from Prosper, TX to McKinney, TX on Highway 380, I was feeling content yet I was concerned that I might have too much—more than my share. I also was worried about what people would think of my good fortune.

The Higher Voice whispered to me and started to explain receiving with this visual in my mind's eye. Like so many other people, I have spent much of my formative years and adult life trying to give from an empty cup.

How can we ever really give in a generous spirit if we haven't received ourselves? In my mind's eye, I saw this amazingly beautiful waterfall. The air reminded me of springtime—fresh, moist, and clean. The sound of the falls hitting the water below was steady and mesmerizing. The sky was clear and the sunlight highlighted the foliage to a vibrant green. There were butterflies in all colors dancing about the tropical flowers.

I was standing in the flow of this waterfall completely at peace and energized. I wanted for nothing. In my hand I held a small silver goblet, trying to catch the water.

There was so much energy and so much water rushing into my cup that it was spilling out as fast as it was rushing in. The water sparkled with white light and jewels. It was rich and abundant. The angels and fairies were there, blessing me and encouraging me to receive more. They were playing in all that was spilling over.

There was no possible way this small chalice would ever be able to contain even a fraction of this flow. It just kept splashing all over the place. It was never ending. It was infinite.

This is exactly how we are when we are standing in the Divine flow of abundance. We can never begin to receive all that is in store for us! So, we can let go of what we have and make room for the next thing, and the next thing and the next thing. Whatever we want is all around each and every one of us.

Of all the lessons in this book, this is one of *the* most important lessons I have to share with you.

at www.TheManifestingMindset.com

For a number of years, I was too giving of my time, money and resources; often at the expense of my children. My entire identity was wrapped up in giving—hoping someday I might receive in return. I thought by giving all of myself, I would be a better person. It was really a way for me to justify my existence. I never really felt like I belonged anywhere; such a strange feeling when I could see that I was loved but felt I had to do so much to earn the love. I certainly didn't want to find out if I wasn't enough!

I always wanted to be a better person and I wanted others to think I was a better person. But what happened all too often is that I would physically wear myself out or become resentful when someone didn't reciprocate--which was often the case.

What God was showing me this day was that if I would fully open myself to receiving, I would eventually overflow into what I call 'Divine giving'.

Divine Giving holds no resentments. **Divine Giving comes from the natural and abundant flow of Universal energy. It is a spill-over of having so**

much love, peace, and joy in your life that you can't help but give it away--no strings attached.

Any kind of giving that is not from this overflow of receiving is inauthentic. It usually comes with stipulations, conditions and/or expectations of what has to be given in return. That really is not a gift at all.

In receiving to overflowing, no matter how much we receive, we could never take away from anyone else. There is so much of everything that we could never even begin to deplete it. It is a renewable resource.

If you are someone who feels like you give too much or not enough, turn off the spigot of giving. We cannot give and receive at the same time. If you notice that there is a phone call you don't want to take, then don't take it. If you are giving someone your time and energy out of guilt, stop!

Instead, turn on the receiving spigot. Start saying, "Yes!" more, when someone offers to help you. Notice how that feels. And, while we are at it, stop apologizing when you do receive something. A simple, "Thank you!" is more than enough.

The shower is an excellent place to practice receiving. When we get into the shower, we are naturally in a receiving mode. We step into the shower to energize ourselves. We 'take' a shower. We fill our cup to overflowing. We aren't trying to do or give anything to anyone else but ourselves. We are there totally to receive, refresh and rewind. Have you ever wondered why you do your best thinking in the shower? It is because you are open to receiving. You are more open to hearing that Higher Voice because you are relaxed and happy. We can tune out of the world and tune in to ourselves.

Strategy:
Receive to Overflowing

Go outside now or as soon as you can and sit (or lay down) with your face toward the sun. Mentally, physically, emotionally and spiritually absorb as much of the sun's light on your face, your arms, your chest, your legs, etc. Absorb as much you can. Feel the energy. See the energy cleansing and renewing your spirit. Take in as much as you want. See how much you can absorb fully into your soul.

Now, in doing this, is there any possible way to take so much energy from the sun that someone else would be left without the sun? Did your neighbor, your child, your friend or anyone else go without the sun because you took too much?

That would be ridiculous, right?

Well, God's abundance for us is like that. There is so much and it is so vast and infinite that we can't even scratch the surface of having too much. RECEIVE!.

at www.TheManifestingMindset.com

Manifesting Secret #5

TAKE INSPIRED ACTION

"It is in the compelling zest of high adventure and of victory, and in creative action, that man finds his supreme joys."

~Antoine de Saint-Exupery

The moment you ask for something that you desire, Divine Guidance will speak to you through your intuition, gut feelings and inspiration. Listen to these feelings because you will be led directly towards what you desire as soon as you ask for it.

Moving forward with these hunches (even when it doesn't make logical sense) is inspired action. Inspired action comes from that inner knowing and taking action in accordance with that Higher Voice.

If you haven't followed your gut instincts much or it may have been a long time since you did, this inspiration or feeling to do something may seem very illogical to you. Now, if you keep getting this distinct feeling you should do something, then listen and take that action.

Following inspiration is the quickest route to manifesting; it produces miraculous results with minimal effort!

I learned from Rhonda Britten, author of *Fearless Living*, that when we hear this voice that inspires us to do something, this voice (the true voice of God) will never put a time limit on anything or rush you in any way--but you have free will to assign a time frame for yourself.

Also, don't assume that just because you hear the voice of God or your Divine Guidance Team and follow your gut instincts to do something, that you will be 100% successful. Sometimes this voice does not lead us to success.

This was an 'ah-ha' moment for me. I thought if I followed the voice of my Divine Guidance Team that I was <u>guaranteed</u> success. Not so.

What happens is that when we take a step towards our vision, we will receive inspiration for the next right action. However, if we stop taking inspired action because we think God or the Universe has us 100% covered (So, we just sit back and relax…), then the next right action will not reveal itself and eventually the opportunity will disappear. This is a team effort!

You take action, ask your Divine Guidance Team to help and then continue to work together towards fulfillment of what you desire. It just makes sense.

Manifesting prosperity (or manifesting anything for that matter) requires action—and not

just any action—inspired action. We have to take consistent, deliberate, inspired action to manifest what we desire.

Many times we think we are just going to think about it or visualize it and it will appear but that's not the case. What will happen is that you will start receiving inspired ideas about which actions to take and insights of what needs to happen. You begin to orchestrate this incredible game of manifesting through Clarity of Intention and Asking for What You Want. However, if you don't follow through with Receiving or Taking Inspired Action, you are going to stall out.

Working hard should not be confused with taking Inspired Action.

Working hard separates us from the natural, abundant flow of the Universe. Hard work can distract us to the point that we often miss what we want even when it passes right by us.

Inspired action is taking action in the flow. It gives us energy.

We want to stay relaxed and aware to what's already coming our way so we can move with it. When we are calm and listening to our intuition, we can sense what's already there and feel if it resonates within us in a good way to forward towards what we want.

Inspired action is the physical energy needed to manifest in the physical plane here on Earth.

Many times, we are too busy working hard for what we ask for, rather than relaxing and listening to the whisper and allowing things to come to us in an easier way. Or, we are afraid of change so we don't move towards the very thing we say we want.

Energy is sensitive. More push does not equal more result. More push can sometimes create more resistance. Think of how a tiny drop of water can change the entire ocean.

Strategies:
Take Inspired Action.

Every night before you go to bed or first thing in the early morning, plan your day. Ask yourself a powerful question and listen for the answers. Then promise to take action.

Business: What can I do today to assure I make $20,000 next month? The answers that pop into your head are inspired. PROMISE yourself to take action.

Personal: What are three things I could do today that would bring me greater Joy? Even if it is only 15 minutes, do something that will make you happy on the inside.

What are 3 Key Business Inspired Actions I promise to take today:

1.

2.

3.

What Are 3 Personal Inspired Actions I promise to take today:

1.

2.

3.

Manifesting Secret #5

CELEBRATE

YOUR SUCCESS

"The more you praise and celebrate your life, the more there is in life to celebrate."

~ Oprah Winfrey

Celebrating your success sets you up to have more success in your life. It puts you in the vibrational pull of success.

What we focus on expands.

Keeping a success journal is an easy way to bring your focus to what is working and to create more of that in your life. If you are someone who does an assessment of what didn't get done at the end of the day, then stop that! Instead, focus on the things you did get done and what your accomplishments have been!

Success breeds success.

Most of us have a tendency to focus on what we don't want or what didn't work for us, so we end up feeling like a failure. The Universe says, "Hey, OK. She feels like a failure, so let's bring her more of the same."

When we begin to acknowledge our success, we begin to feel successful. We notice that we really are moving in a positive direction so we begin to lighten up and relax.

When we are relaxed, we open up our receiving mode. Our senses are heightened to more opportunities that are coming our way.

It's also a great time to acknowledge and thank your Divine Guidance Team! They are faithful servants. Can you imagine having a team at the office working diligently for you and you never taking the time to say, "Thank you. That was a great job you did!"?

Or, what if you never said thank you to anyone in your family for their love and support? How long do you think anyone would want to be there for you if you don't take the time to recognize the contribution they make for you?

Celebrating your success joyfully with your Divine Guidance Team acknowledges what is working and what they can do to bring you more of what you want. As you open that communication channel, more messages are received and understood.

Even though our Divine Guidance Team exists in the spiritual realm and they would do absolutely anything for us, they need to be acknowledged for a job well done. It's so important to do that.

Opening up to this relationship feels childlike to me. Maybe there is some similar past experience I had with my angels as a child that I have long forgotten. Whatever it is, it puts me in a state of joy. Always acknowledge what is working on paper or speak it out loud with a resounding, "I am grateful for..." or "Thank you for..."-- And finish with an "Amen."

Remember to have fun and play. Joy is the highest vibration and attracts the best to us!

Strategies:
Celebrate Your Success

Keep a Success Journal. Any spiral notebook or journal can be used as a Success Journal. You can acknowledge any success no matter if it is teeny-tiny or great big.

Example: If you want to create more money in your life and you find a penny and put it in your piggy bank, that would be a success! The more you acknowledge what is working, the more and more things you will have working in your favor!

1. Each morning, write at least three successes from the day before

2. Then, write three things you are grateful for. (Choose something different every day.)

Join The Manifesting Mindset Mastermind

BONUS Manifesting Secret

THE MANIFESTING PROSPERITY ATTUNEMENT

"Affirmation without discipline is the beginning of delusion."

~ Jim Rohn

Traveling hundreds of miles from show to show with the pillow company provided plenty of windshield time to think about what I really wanted my life with my kids to be like.

I was receiving many messages from my Divine Guidance Team including powerful questions and affirmations that I had never heard of before.

One day, I heard the question, "What would you do if you had everything you ever wanted?" It struck a chord with me so I wrote in on many notes and hung it everywhere I could!

What would you do if you had everything you ever wanted?

This is an incredibly powerful question that I still ask myself. It has a way of tricking our mind with a question on the assumption that we have everything we want. So, what we begin to see in our life is what we want! It is brilliant!

Some of these affirmations became the Manifesting Prosperity Attunement™ that has hung on my bathroom mirror ever since.

The Manifesting Prosperity Attunement™ begins to shift your vibration to receive positive events into your life. Make copies and place this attunement on your mirror, in your car, on your refrigerator, and by your bedside. Every sentence is powerful.

Write it in your shower with a dry erase marker.

It's best to activate your subconscious mind first thing in the morning when you are relaxed and in a receiving mode—like in the shower.

at www.TheManifestingMindset.com

Today is my day. I AM UNLIMITED.

I have more than enough time, money, and energy to do what I want, when I want.

I AM A RECEIVER. Receiving expands the highest vibration that I AM and brings me peace, joy, and love. I receive to overflowing!

I have decided that it is important that I feel good. I continually choose ways, thoughts and experiences that make me feel the best that I am.

Today is my day. I can do anything.

Absolutely ANYTHING.

Join The Manifesting Mindset Mastermind

THANK YOU FOR TAKING THE TIME TO READ THE POWER OF MANIFESTING

 I would absolutely love to hear your stories of manifesting when you use this process. Please feel free to connect with me on Facebook and share your story or ask questions:

www.facebook.com/manifestingengineer

Join a community of others like you who want to create a powerful life to live.

Join The Manifesting Mindset Mastermind

TONJA LOVES TO EDUCATE AND ENTERTAIN YOUR AUDIENCE.

**Why you simply must book
Tonja Waring for your next event.**

♦ The Manifesting Mindset.

Mindset is 99% of Success. Tonja discovered the Manifesting Process™ out of pure desperation. Tonja will grasp the pulse of your audience, connect, and take them on a journey of smashing limitations regardless of circumstances.

at www.TheManifestingMindset.com

◆ Create a Social Profit Company.

Tonja has the gift of blending fundamental business principles with social causes to create greater success for all.   Tonja has been an entrepreneur since she took out her first bank loan at age 16.   Her message is always inspiring and takes CEOs beyond the bottom line to what can be done to create more X's and O's.

◆ The Power of Manifesting Feng Shui.

Tonja teaches basic feng shui principles any company or individual can use to create a harmonious work environment and home life. She will inspire your audience with the tools, heartset and mindset to impact every facet of their life long after they leave your event.

To order more copies of
The Power of Manifesting, **or to create your own**
business card book, please contact:

TONJA WARING
MANIFESTING PROSPERITY
INTERNATIONAL, LLC

TONJA@TONJAWARING.COM
♦ 972-632-6364 ♦
WWW.TONJAWARING.COM

Tonja speaks at entrepreneurial events, women's
conferences and association events.

Visit her website
www.TonjaWaring.com
to learn more.

Made in the USA
San Bernardino, CA
26 December 2016